1993
Our first Christmas

Darling Scott
To my zeas-sound-Santa
in honor of the first official
celebration

Merry Christmas
your wifely,
Maura
xx

THE

Christmas

BOOK

STUDIO
DESIGNS

FIRST PUBLISHED IN 1992 BY STUDIO DESIGNS, A DIVISION OF
STUDIO EDITIONS LIMITED, PRINCESS HOUSE, 50 EASTCASTLE STREET,
LONDON W1N 7AP, ENGLAND.

PRINTED IN SINGAPORE

COVER: CARRYING HOME THE CHRISTMAS HOLLY,
VICTORIAN BOOK ILLUSTRATION
PRIVATE COLLECTION

ILLUSTRATIONS REPRODUCED COURTESY OF THE BRIDGEMAN ART LIBRARY

Introduction

So many traditions have grown up around Christmas over the centuries, many of them with roots well before the birth of Christ, although it is essentially a Christian festival. It is unknown precisely when Jesus was born but 25 December was chosen as the date because it coincided with an existing pagan festival at the Winter Solstice, an attempt to transform the Pagan festival rather than abolish it. In 601 Pope Gregory instructed Augustine of Canterbury to follow the decoration of pagan temples by that of Churches and to feast at this time: 'Nor let them now sacrifice animals to the devil but . . . for their own eating, and render thanks to the Giver . . . For from obdurate minds it is impossible to cut off everything at once.' By the fourth century 25th December was accepted as Christmas Day.

It was this pagan origin which led to the banning of Christmas as a festival during the sixteenth and seventeenth centuries by the English Puritans. But it is not only the date which lends itself to the Winter Solstice, so many other parts of Christmas do too. The association of both evergreen and candles, for instance, come from these early origins. Evergreen was used to decorate houses and temples in celebration and candles were often given as gifts at this time, beginning a lasting association with light and fire that exists today. The blazing candle which then symbolized warmth and light in the coming year later represented the light of the world and to this day is reflected even onto the Christmas table with the flaming Christmas pudding. The Yule log is another age-old tradition although few fire places would sustain one these days. The Log was brought in on Christmas Eve and kindled with a piece of last year's Log. It was considered unlucky if the Log did not burn for the Twelve Days of Christmas. A remaining piece was then kept until the following year, a charm against fires and lightening and then burned as kindling once more.

Several festivals make up the Christmas period. It begins with Advent on 1st December. Then the 6th December is St Nicholas' Day, which for the Dutch and other countries on the Continent is the day on which the Christmas stocking is delivered by St Nicholas and his dark companion, Black Peter. The 21st December is St Thomas' Day on which collections customarily were made for the poor, followed by Christmas Eve and Christmas Day. It is uncertain why Boxing Day, the day after Christmas, is so called. The most likely explanation is that the Church alms boxes were traditionally opened and distributed on this day, or because tradesmen carried boxes for their Christmas tips on this day. New Year's Eve sees the end of one year and the beginning of the next and then Twelfth Night, 5th January, falls the night before Epiphany, 6 January ending the festive season.

List of Plates

THE REVEREND ROBERT WALKER SKATING
SIR HENRY RAEBURN
National Gallery of Scotland, Edinburgh

Christmas Stockists

dvent begins four weeks before Christmas Day and is the time of preparation. It is in Advent that the decorations appear. As with so much of the Christmas tradition the predominant colour of green has its root in the Pagan Winter Solstice. Evergreen was recognized as the symbol of enduring life and possessed the magic rites of an assurance of the return of vegetation in the coming months. Holly, ivy and mistletoe have remained the favourites to this day, the life-symbols as bearers of fruit in winter. Their associations were strong enough to overcome banning in early Christianity for their paganism, although mistletoe is still rarely found in churches, as the most mystic of the three.

The Christmas tree is a reasonably new addition to the English Christmas. It is thought to have come from Germany where for centuries they have been lit and decorated around advent. The first tree to appear in England was in Queen Caroline's court in 1821. In 1841 Victoria and Albert had a tree at Windsor Castle, thus popularizing the tradition.

TURKEY
NAME/ADDRESS ....

HAM
NAME/ADDRESS ....

STILTON
NAME/ADDRESS ....

SMOKED SALMON
NAME/ADDRESS ....

WINE
NAME/ADDRESS ....

GIFTS
NAME/ADDRESS ....

NAME/ADDRESS ....

NAME/ADDRESS ....

_____
NAME/ADDRESS ....

_____
NAME/ADDRESS ....

MAIL ORDER AND HOME DELIVERIES

TURKEY
NAME .... TELEPHONE ....

HAM
NAME .... TELEPHONE ....

SMOKED SALMON
NAME .... TELEPHONE ....

CHRISTMAS PUDDING
NAME .... TELEPHONE ....

STILTON
NAME .... TELEPHONE ....

CHOCOLATES
NAME .... TELEPHONE ....

FOOD HAMPERS
NAME .... TELEPHONE ....

_____
NAME .... TELEPHONE ....

_____
NAME .... TELEPHONE ....

_____
NAME .... TELEPHONE ....

_____
NAME .... TELEPHONE ....

_____
NAME .... TELEPHONE ....

CHARITIES
NAME .... TELEPHONE ....

NAME .... TELEPHONE ....

NAME .... TELEPHONE ....

NAME .... TELEPHONE ....

NAME .... TELEPHONE ....

Caterers and Domestic Staff

NAME Los Altos Bartending .... TELEPHONE ....

COMMENT '93 $100/4 hrs. Wendy - quiet & competent - next time pass drinks

NAME MacArthur Park   '93 .... TELEPHONE ....

COMMENT Ahi Tuna - rave reviews! mozzarella tomato - out! cheese basket - out!

NAME .... TELEPHONE ....

COMMENT ....

NAME .... TELEPHONE ....

COMMENT ....

NAME .... TELEPHONE ....

COMMENT ....

NAME .... TELEPHONE ....

COMMENT ....

NAME .... TELEPHONE ....

COMMENT ....

NAME .... TELEPHONE ....

COMMENT ....

NAME .... TELEPHONE ....

COMMENT ....

NAME .... TELEPHONE ....

COMMENT ....

NAME .... TELEPHONE ....

COMMENT ....

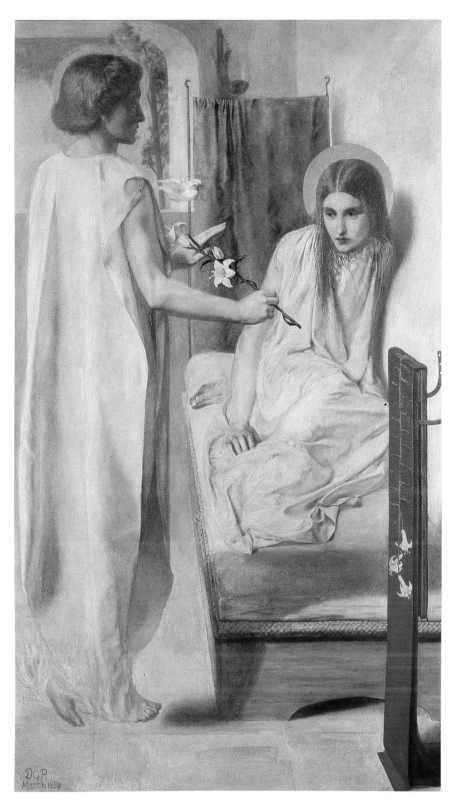

THE ANNUNCIATION
DANTE GABRIEL ROSSETTI
Tate Gallery, London

Essential Shopping List

ALMONDS
BACON
BANANAS
BATTERIES
BRANDY
BRAZIL NUTS
BREAD AND ROLLS

BRUSSEL SPROUTS
BUTTER
CANDIED PEEL
CANDLES
CARROTS
CELERY
CHEESE
CHEESE BISCUITS
CHESTNUTS
CINNAMON
CLINGFILM
CLOVES
COCKTAIL STICKS
COFFEE
COOKING CHOCOLATE
CORIANDER
CRACKERS
CRANBERRIES
CREAM
CRISPS AND SNACKS
CURRANTS, RAISINS,
SULTANAS

DATES
DRIED FRUIT
EGGS
ELECTRICAL PLUGS
FLOUR
FROMAGE FRAIS
GARLIC
GELATINE
GIN
GINGER
GREASEPROOF PAPER

HANGOVER CURES
KITCHEN PAPER
MADEIRA
MARMALADE
MIXED NUTS
MIXED SPICES
MIXER DRINKS
MUSHROOMS
MUSLIN
NUTMEG
OLIVE OIL
ORANGES
ONIONS
PARMESAN CHEESE

PARSLEY
PASTRY
PEPPER CORNS
PORT
POTATOES
RED CABBAGE
REDCURRANT JELLY
RICE
RUM
SALT
SAUSAGES AND SAUSAGE MEAT

SELOTAPE
SHERRY
STOCK CUBES
STRING
SUET
TEA
TIN FOIL
TREE LIGHTS AND SPARE
BULBS
TURKEY
VINEGAR
WINE
WRAPPING PAPER
YEAST
YOGHURT

The Christmas Feast

urkey is a relative newcomer to the Christmas table, quite unknown in Europe before 1542. Of course, the feast itself is as old as the celebration of the Winter Solstice but before 1542 favourites were goose, beef or Christmas pies. In the great houses most popular were bustards, swans, venison, peacocks and the ancient boar's head, the sacred food of the Celt and Norseman.

Perhaps not as ancient as the boar's head, both mince pies and Christmas pudding have been a part of the Christmas feast for centuries. Mince pies were beloved of our sixteenth-century ancestors and it is said that who ever eats one on each of the Twelve Days of Christmas will have twelve happy months. As for Christmas pudding, it has remained virtually the same recipe since 1670.

ROASTING TIMES FOR TURKEY

WEIGHT OF BIRD	METHOD 1 (35°F, 170°C, gas mark 3)	METHOD 2 (425°F, 210°C, gas mark 7)
6–8 lb. (2.5–3.5 kg.)	3–3½ HOURS	2¼–2½ HOURS
8–10 lb. (3.5–4.5 kg.)	3½–3¾ HOURS	2½–2¾ HOURS
10–14 lb. (4.5–6.4 kg.)	3¾–4¼ HOURS	2¾–3 HOURS
14–18 lb. (6.4–8.2 kg.)	4¼–4¾ HOURS	3–3½ HOURS
18–20 lb. (8.2–9 kg.)	4¾–5¼ HOURS	3½–3¾ HOURS
20–24 lb. (9–10.8 kg.)	5¼–6 HOURS	3¾–4¼ HOURS

Allow ¾ lb oven-ready weight per person, 1 lb if the bird is not drawn and trussed.

drawn turkey is usually filled with two different stuffings. The neck end can be stuffed with chestnut or veal forcemeat, and the body cavity filled with a sausage stuffing. An average 12lb. turkey will require a sausage stuffing made from at least 2lb. of sausage meat. Remember not to pack the stuffing too tightly as it will expand during cooking.

Before roasting the stuffed and trussed turkey it should be generously coated with butter all over, seasoned with salt and pepper and then lay the bacon rashers over the breast.

There are two methods for roasting, either quickly in a hot oven or slower. However it is roasted, wrap the bird loosely in foil to prevent it from drying out, opening the foil for the last half an hour to allow the skin to brown. For the slower method the bird should be basted frequently.

CHESTNUT STUFFING FOR TURKEY

INGREDIENTS

2 oz. (50g.) unsalted butter

1 chopped onion

Turkey heart and liver (chopped)

6 oz. (175g.) sliced mushrooms

8 oz. (225g.) chestnut purée

1 small tin pâté de foie gras

2 sticks of celery (chopped)

4 oz. (110g.) chopped bacon

1 level tablespoon chopped parsley

Salt and pepper

2 oz. (50g.) breadcrumbs

Fry the onion, turkey heart and liver and mushrooms in the butter, until this has been absorbed. Stir the chestnut purée with the pâté, and blend in the contents of the pan, with the celery, bacon and parsley. Season and, if necessary, add enough breadcrumbs to bind the stuffing. Fill the breast end of the turkey with the chestnut stuffing and fill the body cavity with sausage stuffing.

SAUSAGE STUFFING

INGREDIENTS

1½ lb. (700 g.) pork sausage meat

4 oz. (110 g.) fresh white breadcrumbs

1 chopped onion

4 oz. (110 g.) minced belly pork

1 beaten egg

Salt and black pepper

Work the breadcrumbs and the onion into the sausage meat, together with the minced pork. Bind the stuffing with the egg and season to taste.

VEAL FORCEMEAT

INGREDIENTS

3 oz. (75 g.) white breadcrumbs

1 oz. (25 g.) butter (melted)

1 small onion

4 oz. (110 g.) lean veal

2 oz. (50 g.) lean bacon

Salt and pepper

1 egg

Stock or water

Mix the breadcrumbs with the butter and blend in the finely chopped onion. Put the veal and bacon through the fine blade of a mincer and add to the breadcrumbs. Season to taste with salt and pepper, then add the lightly beaten egg and enough stock or water to bind the stuffing.

BACON ROLLS

INGREDIENTS

½ lb. (225 g.) streaky bacon

1 oz. (25 g.) beef dripping

Remove the rind and stretch the bacon rashers. Cut each across into two, roll up and secure with wooden cocktail sticks. Fry the bacon in the dripping until crisp, after about 12 minutes. Remove the sticks before serving the rolls.

PORT WINE SAUCE

INGREDIENTS

¼ pint (150 ml.) port

¼ pint (150 ml.) mutton gravy (made from the brown jelly beneath cold mutton dripping and made up to ¼ pint (150 ml.) with boiling water – a beef stock cube may also be used)

1 tablespoon red currant jelly

Salt and pepper

Add the port and red currant jelly to the strained mutton gravy. Bring to the boil and season.

CARRYING HOME THE CHRISTMAS HOLLY
VICTORIAN BOOK ILLUSTRATION
Private Collection

BREAD SAUCE

INGREDIENTS

4 oz. (110 g.) freshly made white breadcrumbs

Whole cloves (number as preferred)

Nutmeg

1 large onion

1 pint (570 ml.) milk

Salt and freshly milled black pepper

Peel the onion and stud it with as many cloves as you wish. Place the onion in a pan with the pint of milk and grated nutmeg and leave to soak for a few hours or over night. Put the pan onto a low heat and stir in the breadcrumbs, salt and pepper. Stir occasionally until the crumbs have thickened into a sauce (about 15 minutes). Remove the onion just before serving.

CRANBERRY SAUCE

INGREDIENTS

1 lb. (450 g.) cranberries

¼ oz. (5 g.) each of root ginger, whole cinnamon and whole allspice

5 cloves

½ pint (275 ml.) cider vinegar

8 oz. (225 g.) Demerara sugar

Put the cranberries in a pan with all the spices tied in muslin. Pour over the vinegar and bring to the boil. Simmer the cranberries until soft and the skins begin to pop, after about 25 minutes. Add the sugar and simmer for a further 20 minutes. Remove the spices and serve cold with roast turkey.

CHRISTMAS PUDDING

INGREDIENTS

8 oz. (225 g.) stoned raisins

1 oz. (25 g.) mixed peel

1 oz. (25 g.) blanched almonds

4 oz. (110 g.) currants

4 oz. (110 g.) sultanas

2 oz. (50 g.) plain flour

¼ level teaspoon ground nutmeg

¼ level teaspoon ground mixed spice

¼ level teaspoon ground cinnamon

½ level teaspoon salt

1 oz. (25 g.) ground almonds

8 oz. (225 g.) shredded suet

4 oz. (110 g.) fresh white breadcrumbs

2 oz. (50 g.) soft brown sugar

3 large eggs

2 tablespoons brandy

¼ pint (150 ml.) milk

1 oz. (25 g.) unsalted butter

Chop the blanched almonds, raisins and mixed peel and mix with the rest of the fruits, salt, spices, sifted flour and ground almonds in a large bowl. When all the fruits are coated mix in the suet, sugar and breadcrumbs, beat the eggs lightly and stir into the mixture. Stir in the milk and brandy until the mixture has a soft consistency.

Butter a 2½ lb. (1 kg.) pudding basin and spoon the pudding mixture into it. Cover the basin with a double layer of buttered grease-proof paper and tie down with a pudding cloth. Place the pudding basin in a large pan of boiling water (two thirds up the side of the basin) and boil steadily for six hours, topping up with water as necessary. Allow the pudding to cool, cover with a fresh cloth and paper and leave to mature in a cool place for at least two months.

On Christmas Day, boil the pudding for a further 4 hours. When ready to serve turn out of the basin, garnish with a sprig of holly, pour over warmed brandy and set alight.

BRANDY BUTTER

INGREDIENTS

3 oz. (75 g.) unsalted butter

3 oz. (75 g.) castor sugar

Grated rind of half orange

2 tablespoons brandy

Cream the butter until soft and pale in colour. Beat in the sugar and orange rind. Gradually beat in the brandy until the mixture is frothy. Chill in the refrigerator until solid.

YULE LOG CAKE

INGREDIENTS

Cake:

8 oz. (225 g.) cooking chocolate

4 tablespoons espresso coffee

2 teaspoons vanilla extract

8 eggs, separated

6 oz. (175 g.) castor sugar

Pinch of salt

Filling:

5 tablespoons butter

4 oz. (110 g.) bittersweet chocolate

1 oz. (25 g.) cooking chocolate

3 eggs, separated

4 oz. (110 g.) castor sugar

3 oz. (75 g.) icing sugar

For the cake: Preheat oven to 375°F, 190°C, gas mark 5. Grease the bottom of a baking tray. Line it with grease proof paper. Combine cooking chocolate and coffee in a small saucepan and melt over very low heat. Add vanilla and remove from the heat. In a large bowl, beat egg yolks with sugar until double in volume. Add the chocolate mixture, folding it in gently. Beat the egg whites with the salt until stiff. Fold them into the chocolate mixture. Bake in the prepared pan for 15 minutes.

When the cake has finished cooking, turn it onto a clean towel. Carefully peel off the paper. Cover the cake with another dry towel, and gently roll up the cake in the towels and set it aside to cool.

For the filling: Combine the butter and chocolates and melt over low heat. Cool. Combine the egg yolks and sugar in a bowl, and beat with an electric mixer, slowly at first and then at high speed, until the mixture thickens. Reduce speed and add the chocolate mixture, mixing till blended. Beat the egg whites until stiff, and at lowest speed, incorporate them into the chocolate mousse. Cool.

When the cake is cooled, gently unroll and spread it with two-thirds of the mousse. Roll cake up again, and place it on a serving plate, seam side down. Ice with remaining mousse. Refrigerate, lightly covered, until 15 minutes before serving. Just before serving, decorate with light dustings of icing sugar.

CHRISTMAS CAKE

INGREDIENTS

1 lb. (450 g.) plain flour

½ level teaspoon salt

1 level dessertspoon mixed spice

1 level teaspoon ground nutmeg

1 level teaspoon ground cinnamon

½ level teaspoon ground cloves

¼ lb. (110 g.) ground almonds

1 lb. (450 g.) currants

1 lb. (450 g.) stoned raisins

1 lb. (450 g.) sultanas

¼ lb. (110 g.) glacé cherries

¼ lb. (110 g.) blanched almonds

¼ lb. (110 g.) whole mixed citrus peel

Rind and juice of a large lemon

12 oz. (350 g.) unsalted butter

10 oz. (275 g.) soft dark brown sugar

8–9 large eggs

8 tablespoons brandy

Almond paste

Royal icing

Butter a 10 in. (25.5 cm) cake tin thoroughly; line it with a double layer of greaseproof paper brushed with melted butter. Tie a double layer of brown paper round the outside of the tin, allowing it to protrude well above the rim – this prevents the Christmas cake burning.

Sift all the dry ingredients – flour, seasoning, spices and ground almonds – together into a large bowl. Mix in all the finely chopped fruits and the chopped almonds. Blend thoroughly.

Cream together, in a separate bowl, the sugar, butter and grated lemon rind, until fluffy. Beat in 8 eggs, one at a time. Stir this into the flour and fruit mixture, followed by the lemon juice and 4 tablespoons of brandy. The mixture should be soft and moist. If necessary add the remaining egg beaten with a little milk.

Spoon the cake mixture into the prepared tin, level the top and bake the cake on the shelf below the centre of a pre-heated oven, at 250°F 130°C (mark ½), for 1 hour. Reduce the heat to 225°F, 120°C (mark ¼) and bake for a further 3½–4 hours. The cake is done when it begins to shrink from the sides.

Remove the cake from the oven, leave to cool slightly before turning it out on to a wire rack to cool. When completely cold, wrap the cake first in greaseproof paper, then in foil, seal tightly and store until six weeks before Christmas. Then, make holes with a skewer in the bottom of the cake and, using a funnel, pour in 4 tablespoons brandy. Reseal and leave until needed for icing.

ROYAL ICING

INGREDIENTS

1 lb. 2 oz. (500 g.) icing sugar, sifted

3 egg whites, size 2

1 teaspoon glycerine

Place the egg whites in a bowl, slowly stir in the icing sugar until the icing falls thickly from the spoon. At this stage whisk with an electric whisk for 10 minutes or until the icing stands up in stiff peaks, then stir in the glycerine.

Now spread the icing all over the base and sides of the cake with a palette knife. Switch to a broad-bladed knife to give a rough finish. Leave the cake overnight for the icing to dry out before placing it in a container till needed.

MINCE PIES

INGREDIENTS

12 oz. (350 g.) shortcrust pastry

1 lb. (450 g.) mincemeat

Milk or egg glaze (optional)

Icing sugar for dusting

Roll out the pastry and use a 3 in. fluted pastry cutter to stamp out 20 rounds and a 2¼ in. fluted cutter to stamp out an equal amount of rounds; re-roll the pastry as necessary. Line 2½ in. wide patty pans with the large rounds and fill to about half their depth with mincemeat. Moisten the underside edges of the smaller rounds and place them, damp side down, over the mincemeat. Press the edges of the pastry lightly together, make a small slit in the top of each pie and glaze with milk or egg white.

Set the patty pans on baking trays and bake just above the centre of a pre-heated oven, at 425°F, (210°C, mark 7) for 20 minutes or until light golden brown.

Remove the mince pies from the tins with a round-bladed knife. Leave to cool on a wire rack and serve warm or cold, dusted with sifted icing sugar.

THE BIRTH OF JESUS
THE MASTER OF OSMA
Osma-Soria Chapter House, Soria

Own Recipes

RECIPE

....

INGREDIENTS

....

....

....

....

....

....

....

....

METHOD

....

....

....

....

....

....

....

....

....

....

....

....

....

....

....

....

....

RECIPE

....

INGREDIENTS

....

....

....

....

....

....

....

....

METHOD

....

....

....

....

....

....

....

....

....

....

....

....

....

....

....

....

....

Own Recipes

RECIPE

....

INGREDIENTS

....
....
....
....
....
....
....
....
....

METHOD

....
....
....
....
....
....
....
....
....
....
....
....
....
....
....
....
....
....
....
....

RECIPE

....

INGREDIENTS

....
....
....
....
....
....
....
....
....

METHOD

....
....
....
....
....
....
....
....
....
....
....
....
....
....
....
....
....
....
....
....

Own Recipes

RECIPE

....

INGREDIENTS

....
....
....
....
....
....
....
....

METHOD

....
....
....
....
....
....
....
....
....
....
....
....
....
....
....
....
....
....
....
....
....

RECIPE

....

INGREDIENTS

....
....
....
....
....
....
....
....

METHOD

....
....
....
....
....
....
....
....
....
....
....
....
....
....
....
....
....
....
....
....
....

DUTCH SCENE IN WINTER
BAREND CORNELIS KOEKKOEK
Private Collection

Festive Drinks

WASSAIL

INGREDIENTS

6 pints (3.5 l.) brown ale

1 lb. (450 g.) soft brown sugar

1 large stick cinnamon

1 level teaspoon grated nutmeg

½ level teaspoon ground ginger

2 lemons, thinly sliced

1 bottle medium dry sherry

Pour 2 pints (1 litre) of the ale into a large pan. Add the sugar and cinnamon stick, and simmer the mixture slowly over low heat until the sugar has dissolved. Add the spices and lemon slices, the sherry and remaining ale.

Before serving the cup, remove the lemon slices.

THE BISHOP

INGREDIENTS

2 lemons

Few cloves

2oz. (50 g.) lump sugar

1½ bottles port or sherry

1 pint (570 ml.) water

Pinch mixed spice

Stab one of the two lemons with cloves and roast in a moderate oven (350°F, 180°C, Gas Mark 4) for 30 minutes. Rub the lump sugar over the remaining lemon to take up the oils from the skin. Place the sugar in a large serving bowl along with the juice squeezed from the lemon. Put the port into a saucepan and bring it almost to the boil. In a separate saucepan bring the water with the spices added, up to the boil. Add the boiling water to the hot port and pour into the serving bowl. Add the roasted lemon and serve as hot as possible.

SPICED CIDER CUP

INGREDIENTS

4 pints (2.25 l.) still dry cider

8 oz. (225 g.) soft brown sugar

20 whole cloves

6 whole cinnamon sticks

16 allspice berries

2 oranges (squeezed)

½ whole nutmeg, grated

8 small apples

2 oz. (50 g.) butter

With a small knife, make a small slit around the middle of each apple, then rub each one with butter. Place them on a baking sheet and bake in the oven for 20–25 minutes 375°F (190°C, gas mark 5) – they should be softened but not floppy, so test them with a skewer. Put all the other ingredients into a large saucepan and heat the mixture, stirring quite often and adding the apples halfway through. Don't let it come right up to the boil, but serve it very hot.

EGGNOG

INGREDIENTS

6 eggs, separated

4 oz. (115 g.) castor sugar

½ pint (275 ml.) thick cream

½ pint (275 ml.) milk

2 tsp. vanilla or rum extract

Grated nutmeg

In a large bowl, beat the egg whites until stiff but not dry, gradually adding the sugar. Beat the yolks in another large bowl until they are lemon yellow. Fold in the egg whites. In a third bowl, beat cream until stiff, then add it to the eggs along with the milk and flavouring, stirring. Chill. Sprinkle with grated nutmeg before serving. (The eggnog may need a gentle stir before serving.)

MULLED WINE

INGREDIENTS

2 bottles full red wine

½ pint (275 ml.) water

¼ pint (150 ml.) orange juice

3 oranges

8–10 cloves

2 lemons

4–6 tablespoons sugar

1 cinnamon stick

Grated nutmeg

2 tablespoons of brandy

Press the cloves into one of the oranges and slice the others and the two lemons. Place all the ingredients into a saucepan and heat until simmering, stirring the sugar until dissolved. Simmer for about half an hour (but do not allow to boil) and serve warm.

CHAMPAGNE CUP

INGREDIENTS

1 bottle champagne

½ teaspoon Maraschino

2 tablespoons brandy

1 lemon

6 lumps of sugar

Cut a few fine strips of lemon peel and place with the brandy and Maraschino. When ready to serve place a sugar lump on the bottom of a champagne glass. Add the brandy and Maraschino to cover the lump of sugar and a piece of lemon peel and then fill the glass with champagne. Serve well chilled.

FRUIT CUP

INGREDIENTS

4 oranges

3 grapefruits

½ pint (275 ml.) grape juice

Mint leaves or fresh basil

Grapes, strawberries, raspberries, slices of lemon

½ pint (275 ml.) sparkling mineral water

Squeeze the oranges and grapefruits and mix with some ice, the grape juice and the mint or basil. Add the fresh fruit and refrigerate. Stir in the mineral water just before serving.

Own Festive Drinks

RECIPE
....

INGREDIENTS
....
....
....
....
....
....
....
....
....

METHOD
....
....
....
....
....
....
....
....
....
....
....
....
....
....
....
....
....
....
....
....
....
....

RECIPE
....

INGREDIENTS
....
....
....
....
....
....
....
....
....

METHOD
....
....
....
....
....
....
....
....
....
....
....
....
....
....
....
....
....
....
....
....
....
....

A WINTER'S DAY IN ST. JAMES' PARK
JOHN RITCHIE
Fine Art Society, London

Left-Over Recipes

TURKEY STOCK

INGREDIENTS

1 turkey carcase (including the skin, stuffing, etc)

1 carrot, split lengthways

1 onion, cut in half

2 celery sticks, cut into chunks

1 sprig thyme

2 bayleaves

10 black peppercorns

Salt

Break the turkey carcase into your largest cooking pot (along with all the bits that cling to it), then add the rest of the ingredients. Cover with water, bring up to simmering point, skim off any scum that rises to the surface, then simmer for 2 hours. After that strain the stock and discard all the debris. The stock will make a delicious base for soups, etc.

CHESTNUT SOUP

INGREDIENTS

1 lb. (450 g.) chestnuts

1 oz. (25 g.) butter

1 onion

2 stalks celery

Generous 2 pints (1.2 l.) turkey stock

Salt and pepper

¼ pint (150 ml.) single cream

Chopped parsley

Cut a slit on the flat side of each chestnut and place them in a saucepan. Cover with boiling water, reboil and simmer for 10 minutes. Drain and peel away both the outer and inner skins.

Melt the butter in a large saucepan. Finely chop the onion and add to the pan. Cover and fry gently for about 5 minutes until tender. Add the chestnuts, the washed and chopped celery and the stock and bring up to the boil. Cover with a lid and simmer gently for 45 minutes to 1 hour, or until the vegetables are quite tender.

Draw the pan off the heat and pass the chestnuts, celery and stock through a sieve, or purée the ingredients in a blender. Return the soup to the pan, season with salt and plenty of freshly milled pepper. Stir in the cream and reheat until hot but not boiling.

Sprinkle with chopped parsley and serve very hot.

STILTON SOUP

INGREDIENTS

2 oz. (50 g.) butter

1 onion, chopped

1 leek, chopped

1 large potato, diced small

1 heaped tablespoon plain flour

1 pint (570 ml.) turkey stock

4 fl oz. (125 ml.) dry cider

4 oz. (110 g.) Stilton cheese, grated

½ pint (275 ml.) milk

1 tablespoon double cream

Salt and pepper

Melt the butter in a thick-based saucepan, then add the prepared vegetables and salt, and cook gently with the lid on for 5–10 minutes. Stir in the flour to absorb the juices and, when smooth, gradually pour in the cider stirring all the time. Now add the chicken stock, cover the pan and simmer gently for 30 minutes. Add the milk and Stilton and re-heat, stirring until the cheese has melted but the soup has not boiled. Taste and season with salt and pepper, then stir in the cream. At this stage you can purée the soup in a food processor or press it through a sieve; or, if you prefer the texture of the chopped vegetables, keep it as it is.

Left-Over Recipes

STILTON RAMEKINS

INGREDIENTS

4 oz. (110 g.) butter

4 oz. (110 g.) flour

1¼ pints (750 ml.) milk

6 eggs, separated

6 oz. (175 g.) Stilton, crumbled

6 oz. (175 g.) parmesan

Cayenne

Salt and pepper

Melt butter and then work in the flour off the heat with a wooden spoon. Stir in the milk to make a thick paste. Heat the mixture, stirring until it thickens to hold the shape of the spoon when pressed (5–8 minutes). Take the pan off the heat, let it cool slightly and then beat in the egg yolks. Stir in the stilton and parmesan and add cayenne, salt and pepper to taste.

Half an hour before serving heat the oven to 375°F. (190°C., gas mark 5). Butter the ramekins and set on a baking tray. Stiffly whip the egg whites. Warm the cheese mixture over a gentle heat to soften. Do not allow to boil. Fold the egg whites into the mixture as lightly as possible. Spoon into the ramekins and bake for 18–20 minutes until puffed and brown. Serve at once.

TURKEY PIE

INGREDIENTS

3½–4 lb. (1½–2 kg.) turkey

1 onion

1 bay leaf

½ level teaspoon salt

5 parsley stalks

Salt and black pepper

½ pint (275 ml.) turkey stock

8 oz. (225 g.) shortcrust pastry (standard recipe)

Egg and milk for glazing

¼ pint (150 ml.) double cream

Chop the turkey into 1 inch (2.5 cms.) pieces. Place in a buttered 2½ pint pie dish, with salt and freshly ground pepper, add the turkey stock.

On a floured surface, roll out the shortcrust pastry to a circle large enough to cover the pie dish. Butter the rim of the dish and line with trimmings of pastry. Damp the edges before covering with the pastry lid. Trim and seal the pastry edges together. Make a few slits in the centre of the pastry to allow the steam to escape, and decorate the pie with leaves cut from the pastry trimmings. Brush the pie with lightly beaten egg, mixed with a few tablespoons of milk.

Bake the pie in the centre of a pre-heated oven, for 25 minutes at 375°F (190°C, gas mark 5). Reduce the heat to 325°F (170°C, gas mark 3) and bake for a further 15 minutes. When ready to serve, cut out a portion of the pastry and pour in the warmed cream. Replace the pastry, sprinkle the pie with chopped parsley and serve.

CHRISTMAS PUDDING WITH DESTINY SAUCE

INGREDIENTS

8 thin slices Christmas pudding

¼ pint (150 ml.) double cream

1 level tablespoon sifted icing sugar

2 tablespoons port

1 oz. (25 g.) unsalted butter

2 level tablespoons castor sugar

Beat the cream until thick, then blend in the icing sugar and port, and chill in the refrigerator until required.

Fry the Christmas pudding in the butter, over medium heat, for 4 minutes, turning once. Arrange the slices on a warm serving dish, dust with the castor sugar and serve the chilled cream in a separate bowl.

Own Left-Over Recipes

NAME

....

INGREDIENTS

....
....
....
....
....
....
....
....
....

METHOD

....
....
....
....
....
....
....
....
....
....
....
....
....
....
....
....
....
....
....
....
....

NAME

....

INGREDIENTS

....
....
....
....
....
....
....
....
....

METHOD

....
....
....
....
....
....
....
....
....
....
....
....
....
....
....
....
....
....
....
....
....

THE ADORATION OF THE SHEPHERDS
PALMA DI VECCHIO
The Prado, Madrid

Menu Planner

Christmas Eve

LUNCH

....

....
....
....

....
....

WINE

....
....

DINNER

....

....
....
....

....
....

WINE

....
....

Menu Planner
Christmas Day

LUNCH

....

....

....

....

....

....

WINE

....

....

DINNER

....

....

....

....

....

....

WINE

....

....

Menu Planner

Boxing Day

LUNCH

....

....

....

....

....

....

WINE

....

....

DINNER

....

....

....

....

....

....

WINE

....

....

Menu Planner
New Year's Eve

LUNCH	DINNER
....	....
....	....
....	....
....	....
....	....
....	....

WINE	WINE
....	....
....	....

Menu Planner
New Year's Day

LUNCH

....

....

....

....

....

....

WINE

....

....

DINNER

....

....

....

....

....

....

WINE

....

....

REMEMBERING JOYS THAT HAVE PASSED AWAY
AUGUSTUS E. MULREADY
Guildhall Art Gallery, London

Games and Entertainment

Music and plays are a central part of Christmas festivities. The churches and streets are full of carols, singers travelling door to door as well as in Church. Many carols have roots in the fourteenth century where they were originally sung as accompaniment to ring-dances. In 1647 the Puritans drove carols out of the Church and from the lives of the educated. Unlike so many things carols did not come back with Charles II and were kept alive only as folk songs. Town waits (watchmen) sang from door to door at Christmas time in return for money and gifts and it is from here that the present day tradition of carol singers comes. By 1822 carols were so near to extinction that collections were made as a record of the past and their general popularity returned.

The oldest forms of Christmas plays were the mummers which have all but died now. Mummers performed masked plays generally as mime. In modern times they have popularly been replaced by the Christmas pantomime.

Entertainment

PLAYS/CONCERTS/PANTOMIMES/CAROL FESTIVALS

YEAR	PERFORMANCE	THEATRE
....	....	....
....	....	....
....	....	....
....	....	....
....	....	....
....	....	....
....	....	....
....	....	....
....	....	....
....	....	....
....	....	....
....	....	....
....	....	....

Games

NAME ....

RULES ....

....

....

....

....

....

....

....

....

....

....

....

....

....

....

....

....

....

....

....

....

PLAYED WITH ....

....

....

Games

NAME ....

RULES ....

....

....

....

....

....

....

....

....

....

....

....

....

....

....

....

....

....

....

....

PLAYED WITH ....

....

....

ADORATION OF THE MAGI
PIETER BRUEGHEL THE ELDER
National Gallery, London

Stocking Fillers

The gift bringer is an age old figure of Christmas and often the first thing a child associates with the time of year. According to different traditions, the gift bringer is now personnified in different ways although his roots are in the same ancient origin. In England Father Christmas is at least fifteenth century as an emblem of festivity. He appeared in early fifteenth century carols but it is not until the nineteenth century that he became the bringer of gifts. His earliest roots are thought to be with Odin the Norse god of war, hence his flowing white hair. His most common saintly association is with St Nicholas, the fourth-century Bishop of Myra who devoted his life to helping the poor. In many parts of Europe St Nicholas (as he is still called) is generally clothed in episcopal robes and mitre, appearing on 6th December (Feast of St Nicholas) or 24th December and is often expected to preach a sermon before distributing gifts.

Shops for Stocking fillers

NAME/ADDRESS ....

....

NAME/ADDRESS ....

....

NAME/ADDRESS ....

....

NAME/ADDRESS ....

....

NAME/ADDRESS ....

....

Stocking

GIVEN	PRESENT	RECEIVED
....	....	....
....	....	....
....	....	....
....	....	....
....	....	....
....	....	....
....	....	....
....	....	....
....	....	....
....	....	....
....	....	....
....	....	....
....	....	....
....	....	....
....	....	....
....	....	....
....	....	....
....	....	....
....	....	....
....	....	....
....	....	....
....	....	....
....	....	....
....	....	....

Stocking

GIVEN	PRESENT	RECEIVED
....	....	....
....	....	....
....	....	....
....	....	....
....	....	....
....	....	....
....	....	....
....	....	....
....	....	....
....	....	....
....	....	....
....	....	....
....	....	....
....	....	....
....	....	....
....	....	....
....	....	....
....	....	....
....	....	....
....	....	....
....	....	....
....	....	....

THE CHRISTMAS TREE
ALBERT CHEVALLIER TAYLER
Private Collection

Presents

The tradition of gifts and greetings began long before Christianity. In pagan Rome rich men were known to give to their poor neighbours at winter solstice, receiving in return garlands of evergreen, or grains of frankincense. Children were traditionally given clay images as a precursor to the doll and men gave each other lamps, symbols of the light of the world and warmth, or money, gold or silver objects for increased wealth in the coming year.

In the early Church this tradition of gift giving was frowned upon. But giving is a natural expression of rejoicing and also a symbol commemorating the gifts of the Magi and by the twelfth century it was usual at Christmas time.

GIVEN	NAME	RECEIVED	LETTER	YEAR
Laura Ashley set	Mom - Rosemary McNulty			
	Margo Harrigan	(Wreath - GIVEN)		'94
Tie COASTERS	Chuck & Ingrid	Serving Pieces		'94
KENDRA SANTA - PLACEMATS		DISH TOWELS		
Alien Gun Conner	Regina	NIGHTGOWN		94
Christmas Throw TAPESTRY		TOWELS BLU + WHI		
coasters		Christmas Dishes		
UMBRELLA, SCARF, PERFUME	Mom	SILK RUNNING SUIT JACKET VELVET		
		NAPKINS - BRIDGE SILVER DUCK PINS		
CHRISTMAS TREE THROW		SILK SET - PANTS BLOUSE		

Presents

GIVEN	NAME	RECEIVED	LETTER	YEAR
....	....	....	....	....
....	....	....	....	....
....	....	....	....	....
....	....	....	....	....
....	....	....	....	....
....	....	....	....	....
....	....	....	....	....
....	....	....	....	....
....	....	....	....	....
....	....	....	....	....
....	....	....	....	....
....	....	....	....	....
....	....	....	....	....
....	....	....	....	....
....	....	....	....	....
....	....	....	....	....
....	....	....	....	....
....	....	....	....	....
....	....	....	....	....
....	....	....	....	....
....	....	....	....	....
....	....	....	....	....

Presents

GIVEN	NAME	RECEIVED	LETTER	YEAR
....	....	....	....	....
....	....	....	....	....
....	....	....	....	....
....	....	....	....	....
....	....	....	....	....
....	....	....	....	....
....	....	....	....	....
....	....	....	....	....
....	....	....	....	....
....	....	....	....	....
....	....	....	....	....
....	....	....	....	....
....	....	....	....	....
....	....	....	....	....
....	....	....	....	....
....	....	....	....	....
....	....	....	....	....
....	....	....	....	....
....	....	....	....	....
....	....	....	....	....
....	....	....	....	....
....	....	....	....	....

Presents

GIVEN	NAME	RECEIVED	LETTER	YEAR
....	....	....	....	....
....	....	....	....	....
....	....	....	....	....
....	....	....	....	....
....	....	....	....	....
....	....	....	....	....
....	....	....	....	....
....	....	....	....	....
....	....	....	....	....
....	....	....	....	....
....	....	....	....	....
....	....	....	....	....
....	....	....	....	....
....	....	....	....	....
....	....	....	....	....
....	....	....	....	....
....	....	....	....	....
....	....	....	....	....
....	....	....	....	....
....	....	....	....	....
....	....	....	....	....
....	....	....	....	....

Presents

GIVEN	NAME	RECEIVED	LETTER	YEAR

THE FLIGHT INTO EGYPT
FRA ANGELICO
Museo di San Marco Dell'Angelico, Florence

Presents

GIVEN	NAME	RECEIVED	LETTER	YEAR

Presents

GIVEN	NAME	RECEIVED	LETTER	YEAR

Presents

GIVEN	NAME	RECEIVED	LETTER	YEAR

CHILDREN WITH A SNOWBALL
ANONYMOUS
British Library, London

Card List

The idea of the Christmas card is little more than a century old. Its origin is thought to be in 'Christmas Pieces' on which school boys wrote their parents greetings to show how their writing was improving. The first recognized card was sent in 1843, designed by JC Horsley. In essence it is an extension of the Christmas present, in sending greetings.

SENT	NAME	RECEIVED	YEAR
	Alex + Kevin Ohlson 2611 Marshall Dr PA 94303		
	Koegels 1960 Clover St Rochester 14618		
	Janice Baer 1280 Colonial Oaks Dr. LA 94024		
	Paul + David Boyers 1397 Lloyd Way MV 94040		
	M/m Robert + Winkles 3500 Darden Road Greensboro NC 27407		

Card List

SENT	NAME	RECEIVED	YEAR
....	....	....	....
....	....	....	....
....	....	....	....
....	....	....	....
....	....	....	....
....	....	....	....
....	....	....	....
....	....	....	....
....	....	....	....
....	....	....	....
....	....	....	....
....	....	....	....
....	....	....	....
....	....	....	....
....	....	....	....
....	....	....	....
....	....	....	....
....	....	....	....
....	....	....	....
....	....	....	....
....	....	....	....
....	....	....	....
....	....	....	....
....	....	....	....

Card List

SENT	NAME	RECEIVED	YEAR
....	....	....	....
....	....	....	....
....	....	....	....
....	....	....	....
....	....	....	....
....	....	....	....
....	....	....	....
....	....	....	....
....	....	....	....
....	....	....	....
....	....	....	....
....	....	....	....
....	....	....	....
....	....	....	....
....	....	....	....
....	....	....	....
....	....	....	....
....	....	....	....
....	....	....	....
....	....	....	....
....	....	....	....
....	....	....	....
....	....	....	....
....	....	....	....

VIRGIN AND CHILD
TOMMASO MASACCIO
National Gallery, London

Card List

SENT	NAME	RECEIVED	YEAR
....	....	....	....
....	....	....	....
....	....	....	....
....	....	....	....
....	....	....	....
....	....	....	....
....	....	....	....
....	....	....	....
....	....	....	....
....	....	....	....
....	....	....	....
....	....	....	....
....	....	....	....
....	....	....	....
....	....	....	....
....	....	....	....
....	....	....	....
....	....	....	....
....	....	....	....
....	....	....	....
....	....	....	....
....	....	....	....
....	....	....	....
....	....	....	....

Card List

SENT	NAME	RECEIVED	YEAR
....	....	....	....
....	....	....	....
....	....	....	....
....	....	....	....
....	....	....	....
....	....	....	....
....	....	....	....
....	....	....	....
....	....	....	....
....	....	....	....
....	....	....	....
....	....	....	....
....	....	....	....
....	....	....	....
....	....	....	....
....	....	....	....
....	....	....	....
....	....	....	....
....	....	....	....
....	....	....	....
....	....	....	....
....	....	....	....
....	....	....	....

Card List

SENT	NAME	RECEIVED	YEAR
....	....	....	....
....	....	....	....
....	....	....	....
....	....	....	....
....	....	....	....
....	....	....	....
....	....	....	....
....	....	....	....
....	....	....	....
....	....	....	....
....	....	....	....
....	....	....	....
....	....	....	....
....	....	....	....
....	....	....	....
....	....	....	....
....	....	....	....
....	....	....	....
....	....	....	....
....	....	....	....
....	....	....	....
....	....	....	....

SKATERS IN THE BOIS DE BOULOGNE
PIERRE AUGUSTE RENOIR
Private Collection

Photograph Gallery

YEAR ....

YEAR ....

Photograph Gallery

YEAR ....

YEAR ....

Photograph Gallery

YEAR ....

YEAR ....